W9-CJD-027

The Conflict Resolution Library™

Dealing with Being the Middle Child in Your Family

• Elizabeth Vogel •

The Rosen Publishing Group's
PowerKids Press™
New York

12172375

For Heather Feldman, my editor and friend.

Published in 2000 by The Rosen Publishing Group, Inc.
29 East 21st Street, New York, NY 10010

Copyright © 2000 by The Rosen Publishing Group, Inc.

All rights reserved. No part of this book may be reproduced in any form without permission in writing from the publisher, except by a reviewer.

Photo Illustrations by Kristen Artz

First Edition

Layout and design: Erin McKenna

Vogel, Elizabeth.
    Dealing with being the middle child in your family / by Elizabeth Vogel.
            p.   cm. — (The conflict resolution library)
    Includes index.
    Summary: Describes some of the frustrations and benefits that come with being the middle child in a family and offers advice on how to deal with both.
    ISBN 0-8239-5408-0 (lib. bdg.)
    1. Birth order—Psychological aspects—Juvenile literature. 2. Second-born children—Psychology—Juvenile literature. 3. Sibling rivalry—Juvenile literature. [1. Birth order. 2. Brothers and sisters.]   I. Title. II. Series.
    BF723.B5V63 1998
    155.9'24— dc21   98-47368
                                                                                                        CIP
                                                                                                        AC

Manufactured in the United States of America

Contents

The Middle Child

Are you the middle child in your family? This means you have at least one older **sibling** and one younger one. A sibling is a sister or a brother. You have at least two siblings, and maybe you have more. As the middle child, you know what it's like to be older and what it's like to be younger than another sibling. Your younger brother or sister will look up to you as an older sibling, but you also have an older sibling that you look up to. It takes time to figure out your special role in the family.

◀ *Being in the middle means you have older siblings to learn from and younger ones to teach.*

Older Siblings

Your older siblings can be very helpful. They can show you how to do that hard math problem you were given for homework. Your older siblings can also teach you how to play fun games. Older siblings are great with **advice**, too. Sometimes you'd rather talk to your older siblings about a problem than to anyone else. Maybe they faced a similar problem in the past. Your older sisters or brothers can be there for you, to teach you things and help you out. Best of all, your older siblings can be your good friends.

You can always turn to an older sibling for help. ▶

A Family Camping Trip

Darrin's family arrived at the campgrounds for a camping trip. Darrin's older brother, Pete, said, "I'll pitch the tents with Dad!" His younger sister, Maria, said, "I'll gather sticks for the fire." Darrin watched his siblings do their jobs and felt left out. He didn't know what to do. Darrin's mom asked him if he wanted to help her make dinner. Darrin said yes and was a great helper. He even wore the chef's hat his dad had packed. Even though it was hard for him to know what to do at first, Darrin felt good when he found a job he could do well.

◀ *Like Darrin, you might sometimes feel confused about your place in the family. Don't worry. You'll find out where you fit in.*

Younger Siblings

Younger sisters and brothers are fun to have around. They look up to you and admire you. They will often be your biggest fans. Little siblings are happy to go along with your new ideas or projects. If you know how to play cards, you can teach your little brother how to play. You can also help him study for his science test in school. As an older sibling, you can lend your little siblings your favorite books. They'll enjoy the books even more if you read with them. Little sisters and brothers love spending time with you.

Having a younger sibling means you have someone who looks up to you. ▶

Sasha and Dominick

Sasha was a middle child, and he often felt left out. His older brother got to be in charge a lot and had a later bedtime. Sasha's younger sister got a lot of attention because she was the baby of the family. Sasha told his parents how he felt. They suggested that he visit his friend, Dominick. Sasha needed to realize that he was important, too. Dominick invited Sasha to play soccer with him. The two friends had fun spending time together. Sasha knew how important he was to Dominick. This made him feel good again.

Spending time with friends is a good way to remember how important you are.

Not Getting Along

Sometimes your siblings might hurt your feelings. Maybe your older sister is being bossy. Your siblings might not be getting along with each other, and you might feel caught in the middle. It is important to share your feelings calmly and directly.

Sisters and brothers sometimes argue. An **argument** is when you disagree about something and get angry. Try to reach a **compromise**. This means both of you try to give in a little.

Sometimes the middle child feels caught in between his siblings. ▶

Denise Discovers Drama

Denise is the middle child of her family. She decides to try out for the school play. "You have a lovely singing voice," her music teacher says. Denise feels special. Her sisters and brothers don't like to sing or act. Denise loves to do both.

Mrs. Jenkins puts the cast list on the bulletin board. "Congratulations," she tells Denise. Denise has a great part in the play. She is so excited to perform on stage for her family and the whole school.

◄ *Denise's family is proud of her special talents. Denise is proud too.*

What About Me?

Do you ever feel left out because you're the middle child? Sometimes being in the middle can be **frustrating**. When you feel upset, tell your parents. They can help you. Another **solution** is to spend time with friends. Friends can cheer you up and make you smile.

Another way to handle feeling left out is to spend time finding out what you like to do. Do you like to sing or dance or play sports? Getting to know your **unique** talents will help you feel special throughout your whole life.

Hanging out with friends is a fun way to learn new things. ▶

Time to Talk

It's a good idea to share your feelings with your parents. They can help you if you have a problem. Set aside some time to spend alone with your parents. This is a good opportunity to let them know how you are doing. Maybe you want to tell them about a great book that you have read. Or maybe you want to tell them about the new friend you made in school. Your parents want to know how you are doing. Watching their middle child grow up is one of their greatest pleasures.

◀ *Talk to your family if you're feeling left out.*

The Best of Both Worlds

Being the middle child in your family can make you feel very special. You are both an older sibling and a younger one. Your little siblings **rely** on you, and your older siblings enjoy helping you out when you need them.

Your **experiences** can teach you a lot about yourself and other people. Lots of middle children end up having many good friendships because they know how to deal well with people. You should feel proud of being the middle child in your family!

Glossary

advice (ed-VYS) An opinion about how to handle a problem.

argument (AR-gyoo-mint) When two people who don't agree about something get angry with each other.

compromise (KOM-pruh-myz) When people work out an argument by each giving in a little.

experience (ik-SPEER-ee-ints) An event in someone's life.

frustrating (FRUS-tray-ting) When not being able to change a situation makes you feel angry or sad.

rely (rih-LYE) To depend on something or someone.

sibling (SIH-bling) A person's sister or brother.

solution (suh-LOO-shun) An answer to a problem.

unique (yoo-NEEK) One of a kind.

Index